U.S. MARINE CORPS

FIGHTING FORCES

JASON COOPER

Rourke
Publishing LLC
Vero Beach, Florida 32964

www.rourkepublishing.com

PHOTO CREDITS: title page, pp. 9, 11, 15, 16, 19, 20 courtesy Defense Visual Information Center; p. 5 courtesy U.S. Navy; pp. 6, 13, 23, 24, 26, 27, 28 courtesy of National Archives.

Title page: *A Marine lowers himself down a 70-foot (21-meter) cliff during an exercise.*

Editor: Frank Sloan

Cover and page design by Nicola Stratford

Library of Congress Cataloging-in-Publication Data

Cooper, Jason, 1942-
U.S. Marine Corps / Jason Cooper.
v. cm. — (Fighting forces)
Includes bibliographical references and index.
Contents: What the Marine Corps does — The U.S. Marine Corps at work — The Marine Corps Command — Life in the Marine Corps — Marine Corps weapons — The Marine Corps up to today.
ISBN 1-58952-715-1 (hardcover)
1. United States. Marine Corps—Juvenile literature. [1. United States. Marine Corps.] I. Title. II. Series: Cooper, Jason, 1942- Fighting forces.

VE23.C74 2003
359.9'6'0973—dc21

2003005285

Printed in the USA

CG/CG

Table of Contents

What the Marine Corps Does

CHAPTER ONE

The proud United States Marine Corps is known for taking on tough, dangerous jobs in war. The Marine Corps is one of America's **armed services**. Its overall job is to defend the nation. It shares that task with its sister services, the Air Force, Army, Navy, and Coast Guard.

The Marines, however, have a special role to play. They are trained to fight on land after arriving by sea. That's why the Marines are called an **amphibious** force. Of course, not all Marine **operations** begin at sea. Marines also enter battles by air or land.

▲ *A Marine amphibious assault vehicle splashes ashore during training exercises on Tinian Island.*

▲ *Distant, difficult places are nothing new for Marines. Here Marines collect Viet Cong prisoners near Cho Lai, Vietnam, in August, 1965.*

Over the years battle-ready Marines have usually been the nation's go-to force. Being the first American force sent to face an enemy in battle is nothing new. By the 1840s, the Marines had seen **combat** in places most Americans had never heard of. "The Marine Corps Hymn" recalls early Marine battles "From the Halls of Montezuma to the Shores of Tripoli." The Marines entered Mexico City (once the home of emperor Montezuma) during the Mexican War (1846-1848). They fought in Derna, Tripoli (now Libya), in 1805.

Marines call themselves "the few, the proud." Marine strength in numbers has always been fairly small. In the early 2000s the Marine Corps had a force of about 170,000 on active duty. It had about 30,000 in **reserve**.

FACT FILE ★

THE MARINES ARE A CLOSE, EXTREMELY PROUD SERVICE. READ THIS PART OF "THE MARINE CORPS HYMN:"

IF THE ARMY AND THE NAVY
EVER LOOK ON HEAVEN'S
SCENES
THEY WILL FIND THE
STREETS ARE GUARDED
BY UNITED STATES
MARINES

CHAPTER TWO

THE U.S. MARINE CORPS AT WORK

The Marines' main job is to attack and take enemy positions. Marines are trained in all kinds of environments. They expect to be the first **troops** in a battle zone, wherever it may be. And in almost every major war of the United States, they have been. They are also specially trained to make shore landings from boats. Small groups of Marines often move into an area ahead of other troops. If the enemy has a strong position, the Marines are often the first to know.

Marine units are always ready to travel, even with little warning. Problems in other nations may spring up without warning. Some of those situations can turn into problems for the United States or her interests. In those cases, the Marines may be sent in. The Marines can sometimes solve a problem just by showing up. At other times the Marines have to use force.

▲ *Marines train on the desert sands of Kuwait.*

Marine Forces

Division	16,000 marines
Regiment	2,250 marines
Battalion	750 marines
Company	150 marines
Platoon	42 marines
Squad	13 marines
Fire Team	4 marines

The Marines work closely with the U.S. Navy. Navy warships and amphibious boats carry Marines. Marine troops are used to protect the Navy's bases. Marines also guard many important American places, including the White House and the U.S. Naval Academy at Annapolis, Maryland.

The Marines are not entirely a band of **infantry** fighters. The Marine Corps also has an air unit. Marine pilots fly the same type of aircraft as the Navy.

HIGHEST RANKS
IN DESCENDING ORDER

- GENERAL
- LIEUTENANT GENERAL
- MAJOR GENERAL
- BRIGADIER GENERAL
- COLONEL
- LIEUTENANT COLONEL
- MAJOR
- CAPTAIN
- FIRST LIEUTENANT
- SECOND LIEUTENANT

The fight against terrorism brought Marines to Afghanistan in 2001.

CHAPTER THREE

The Marine Corps Command

Each of the American armed services is under the command of **civilians**. Civilians are people who are not part of the armed services.

All of America's armed services, except the Coast Guard, are part of the Department of Defense. Within that department are more departments, such as the Department of the Navy.

The Department of the Navy includes both the U.S. Navy and the Marine Corps. The civilian leader of the Department of Defense is the head of both the Navy and Marines.

FACT FILE ★

THE FINAL SAY IN **MILITARY** DECISIONS BELONGS TO THE PRESIDENT. THE PRESIDENT, ALSO A CIVILIAN, IS THE COMMANDER-IN-CHIEF OF ALL THE AMERICAN ARMED FORCES.

In turn, the Department of the Navy is headed by a civilian secretary of the Navy. The top-ranking Marine has the title of commandant of the Marines. He is chosen by the president of the United States. He reports to the secretary of the Navy.

▲ *In the Philippine Islands, General Douglas MacArthur splashes ashore as commander of American forces in the Pacific during World War II.*

CHAPTER FOUR

LIFE IN THE MARINE CORPS

Marine recruits are those men and women who have agreed to join the Marine Corps. They are between the ages of 17 and 28 and **enlist** for a period of three, four, or six years. Some Marines make a long-term career of the Corps.

Marine recruits train either at Parris Island, South Carolina, or at the Marine base in San Diego, California. Basic training at the Marine "boot camp" lasts 12 weeks. During basic training, recruits learn to be Marines. They learn how to use weapons, obey orders, and follow Marine traditions. They also undergo a tough physical fitness program.

A Marine training in swamp water slips under barbed wire. ▶

▲ *A Marine trained in Special Operations uses binoculars in Kandahar, Afghanistan. The tape reduces the sun's brightness.*

Officers are those Marines with the rank of Lieutenant or higher, such as Major, Colonel, and General. Some Marine officers come from the U.S. **Naval** Academy. The Naval Reserve Officers Training Corps (NROTC) trains college students to be Marine officers.

A few select Marines belong to special Marine Reconnaissance units. These men are trained in operations that require a small, highly skilled force. Marine Recon is often used with Special Operations forces, like the Navy SEALS, of the other services.

MARINE CORPS WEAPONS

CHAPTER FIVE

The Marine Corps uses a great variety of weapons. A Marine's basic weapon is an M16A2 rifle.

Marine artillery groups use several kinds of big guns that fire explosive shells long distances. Some of these guns are **howitzers** and **mortars**. Marine units also have several types of **missiles**. Marines fire the Redeye and Stinger missiles from their shoulders.

Marine armored units operate at least six different kinds of tank-like vehicles. Marine aircraft lend air support to ground forces. They also support Navy operations. The Marines' main fighter jet is the F-18 Hornet. One of its jobs is to knock out enemy planes in any kind of weather. The Hornet also attacks ground targets. It can be fitted with several kinds of missiles. These fighters can fly from land bases or from Navy aircraft carrier decks.

▲ *A Marine armed with an M-16 rifle trains at the Jungle Warfare Training Center on Okinawa, Japan.*

▲ *Marines watch their TOW missile scream toward a training target in Kuwait.*

The Marine AV-8B Harrier II is an all-weather plane. It carries guns and missiles to destroy enemy targets day or night.

In the early 2000s the Marine Corps was hoping to add the MV-22 Osprey to its weapons list. The Osprey, however, was proving difficult to fly. The Osprey is a highly unusual aircraft. It can take off by lifting straight up, like a helicopter. It can land the same way. But once in the air, the Osprey cruises like an airplane! The Osprey would be useful both as a troop transport and as an attack aircraft. The Marines hope to use the high-tech Osprey to replace some of their old helicopters.

FACT FILE ★

THE MARINE CORPS ALSO HAS SEVERAL DIFFERENT TYPES OF HELICOPTERS. THEY CAN FIRE GUNS AND ROCKETS, PERFORM RESCUE MISSIONS, AND MOVE TROOPS.

CHAPTER SIX

The Marine Corps Up to Today

The U.S. Marine Corps arrived before the Declaration of Independence. The Continental Congress set up two groups of riflemen as Marines on November 10, 1775. America's Declaration of Independence from England followed on July 4, 1776.

After the Revolutionary War (1775-1783) and their later success in Tripoli, the Marines fought in the War of 1812 (1812-1815). Marines helped Andrew Jackson's Army troops defeat the British in the Battle of New Orleans. The Marines were in action again during the Mexican War (1846-1848). They landed on both coasts.

FACT FILE ★

MARINES FOUGHT AGAIN FOR UNION FORCES IN AMERICA'S CIVIL WAR. THEY FOUGHT BOTH LAND AND NAVAL BATTLES.

▲ *An old painting shows a general with his Marines entering Mexico City in September, 1847.*

Marines were called to defend American interests in China several times during the late 1800s and early 1900s. They entered Latin America several times, too, between the 1880s and 1933. These actions were in such places as Panama, Nicaragua, Haiti, and the Dominican Republic.

▲ *U. S. Marine patrol boats float on the Ozoma River, Santo Domingo City, while on duty in 1919.*

The Marine Corps was a big part in the fight against Japanese forces in the Pacific during World War II (1939-1945). Marines invaded Japanese-held Guadalcanal in August, 1942. That was the first time the United States went on the attack in the Pacific. The Japanese attacked American ships at Pearl Harbor, Hawaii, in late 1941. The attack had badly hurt America's ability to fight in the Pacific.

General Holland Smith sent the Marines westward one island at a time. They skipped some islands. The Marines called their plan "island hopping." Marines with Navy and sometimes Army support fought their way across the central Pacific. They moved closer and closer to Japan.

FACT FILE ★

THE UNITED STATES ENTERED WORLD WAR I (1914-1918) IN 1917. MARINES WERE ON THE FIRST U.S. TROOPSHIPS TO REACH EUROPE.

In February and March, 1945, Marines battled Japanese soldiers on the island of Iwo Jima. America needed the airplane runways on Iwo Jima for air strikes against Japan. America also needed to stop Japanese planes from using the runways.

▲ *Marines raise the American flag on the heights of Iwo Jima on February 23, 1945.*

Iwo Jima was the largest all-Marine battle ever. About one of every three Marines at Iwo Jima was either killed or wounded. More than 6,800 Marines died in the battle for this 8-mile square- (21 square kilometers-) island. The Marines had to kill almost every Japanese soldier on the island—more than 22,000.

In April, 1945, Marines landed on the

island of Okinawa. They played a big part in another costly American victory. The landing at Okinawa of Army and Marine troops was the largest sea landing of the Pacific war. American ships sent a hurricane of gunfire onto Japanese positions. But the Japanese had dug into caves and tunnels. Marine and Army troops lost about 8,000 young men on Okinawa. The Japanese lost more than 100,000.

▲ *A Marine looks for hidden Japanese riflemen from the entrance to a cave on Okinawa in 1945.*

▲ *Marines hike forward near icy Hugaru-ri, Korea, on the day after Christmas, 1950.*

The Marines fought in the icy winters of Korea during the Korean War (1950-1953). About 450,000 Marines served in the Vietnam War (1957-1975).

Marines were sent to Lebanon and Grenada in the 1980s. Marines fought in the Persian Gulf War (1991) and were sent to Bosnia-Herzegovina and Serbia later in the 1990s. Marine units also landed in Rwanda, Sierra Leone, and Somalia in the l990s.

In 2001, Marines were sent to Afghanistan to help destroy terrorist camps and remove the Taliban government from power. During Operation Iraqi Freedom in 2003, Marines played a major role in America's successful effort to attack and remove Saddam Hussein's government.

In many ways the U.S. Marines of the future will be no different than the Marines of the past.

Glossary

amphibious (am FIB ee us) — of use both on land and sea

armed services (AHRMED SUR viss ez) — the military forces of a government, such as the U.S. Marine Corps

civilians (suh VILL yunz) — people who are not members of the armed forces

combat (COM bat) — warfare; fighting with violence

enlist (en LIST) — to join an armed service

howitzers (HOW it zuhrz) — short cannons that fire explosives; types of artillery weapons

infantry (IN fun tree) — soldiers on the ground; foot soldiers

military (MIL uh tare ee) — having to do with or being part of the nation's armed forces

missiles (MISS uhlz) — weapons projected to strike distant objects

mortars (MOR tuhrz) — firing devices, such as cannons

naval (NAY vuhl) — having to do with a navy

operations (op urh AY shunz) — particular jobs or missions carried out by an armed service

reserve (ree ZURV) — the non-active soldiers who may be called to active duty in a national emergency

troops (TROOPZ) — soldiers, or groups of soldiers

INDEX

FURTHER READING

Aaseng, Nathan. *The Marine Corps in Action*. Enslow, 2001

Bradley, James and Ron Powers. *Flags of Our Fathers: Heroes of Iwo Jima*. Bantam Doubleday Dell Books for Young Readers, 2001

WEBSITE TO VISIT

www.usmc.mil

ABOUT THE AUTHOR

Jason Cooper has written several children's books about a variety of topics for Rourke Publishing, including the recent series *Eye to Eye with Big Cats* and *Holiday Celebrations*.